From Soul to Paper

Krisel Qurku

Copyright © 2012 Krisel Qurku

From Soul to Paper

Perspective Press Global Ltd

All rights reserved.

ISBN: 978-1-914275-00-5

DEDICATION

I want to dedicate this book to everyone who helped me make it a reality.

To my family who has endorsed my decision from the very beginning. To my parents, for loving and supporting me through any hardships in my extraordinary journey. To my little sister, Emi, who knew before everyone else did and who has been even more excited for this book than I ever was. Surely, to the rest of my relatives, aunts, uncles, cousins, grandparents who I wish to make proud with this book.

To my friends with whom I created the experiences that I have written about. To those who have been there for me through everything, who have made me cry tears of joy and been a shoulder to cry on through the tears of pain. I will always be thankful and hope that our friendship will continue to be just as strong in the future.

Lastly, to all my readers. Without you, this book would be worthless. You are what gives it meaning and beauty. I hope you flip through the pages with sparks in your eyes and smiles in your faces.

AM I A WRITER

I am not a writer,
Even though I write,
For I have not perfected the virtuosity of the art.

I am just a dainty dreamer,
Gush of lines and stories of worries,
Spurting through my fingers,
Loaded with troubles or glories.

I am just a little dreamer,
Who sometimes cannot dream,
With anguish holding me down,
Tossed out of my realm.

I am just an elfin dreamer,
Standing in a corner,
Trying to fully pick up a melody,
Captivated as it gets warmer.

No, I am not a dancer,
Nor a singer,

I am just a dreamer,
Inelegantly moving my limbs,
Espying the champions on the podium,
Seeking to catch a glimpse.

Some might not appreciate this effort,
I have not learned the steps or lines,
Nor am I good,
I just clumsily sway,

Under the spell of the tune.

ECHOING

I hear a ringing in my ears,
Green and turquoise soundwaves,
Beautifully in harmony,
Could you speak up?
I can't hear,
I keep hearing those words,
Floating, circling,
Captivating my mind,
Those cerulean vibrations,
A sedative vibration,
That I can hear,
See,
Feel,
When I was here,
Reminiscing their whispers,
Of mysteries,
And promises,
Getting louder and louder,
Too loud,
To be ignored,
Forget this empty noise,
For I know it won't be long,
Until it comes again,
A lilac pulse,
Filled with reassurance,
As I know it's reminding of my worth,
And then I draw blank,
The sound I can thank.

LONELINESS

I am not alone,
But I feel lonely.
Some people know me,
Yet nobody knows me.
I overhear screams,
But they're so silent,
A series of dreams,
Unspeakably violent.
I feel like a ghost,
But I haven't died yet.
Thoughts go from pillar to post,
Still, it's sort of quiet.
It's the pain of loneliness,
Coming in soothing whispers,
In fatigue voices,
Sending shivers,
Until the soul rejoices,
Coming in roaring silence,
In docile screeches,
I drop my life,
Unable to find the pieces.

WRITER'S BLOCK

Whenever I grab my pen,
Millions of ideas start flowing in my head,
But words give up in front of ideas,
And there I stand with my page blank.

I can feel the rhymes abandoning me,
The rhythm has left,
But I keep knitting lines together,
Making them make sense.

My right says to my left,
"don't think too much, just write"
But I'm thinking in lowercase,
Nothing capital stands out right.

How can I get out,
Of this fog of raw dullness,
This constant push and pull,
And wake up from this numbness.

SPRINKLING SPIRIT

The old paths,
Covered by flowers,
Parsley green fields,
Shine in sunny hours.,
Chirping chicks,
Filling the sky,
Staffs of slim light,
Start beaming from up high.
Clouds like tufty pillows,
Glide across the horizon,
Carrying an airy drizzling rain,
The flora it's energizing.
Cleansing the land,
And banishing the coldness,
Plinking off the leaves,
To beauty it has proneness.
Its liquid grace,
Baptized a whole world,
Aromas hovering in the air,
As butterflies' whirl.
Celestial red valerian sprouts,
Bright tulips before our eyes,
Daffodils bloom in the fields,
Jewel green grasshoppers,
Jump atop the grass.
The sunrise chorus
Is the highlight of spring,
A melodious blackbird,
Such an astonishing thing.
The world is lush,
Young and bountiful,

A spirit enriching thing,
Taken over by a wrath silver moon.

A BOWL FULL OF BLISS

The soft yet crispy pitter patter of rain on my skin,
Water hitting the grounds mixed with the noise of the night
Gazing at the horizon then closing my eyes...

When I enter the house
And I'm struck by the paradisaical scent of freshly baked cookies
Mouth-watering, no doubt.

When I open a brand-new book
And drag it towards my face
And smell its woodsy pulp with an awed look.

When days start to stretch into sunset
Swirls of pink and orange fade into blue and purple
A ravishing sight, hard to forget.

The small things are so much bigger than the great things
As I make fun of what sadness brings
While I relish little moments full of bliss.

LIKE THE SEA

It's not often you get to see,
A sunrise gold beach,
For I have the privilege to gaze,
At the calm, slothful sea.
The pulse of this dreamy sea,
Is unlike any part of nature,
Its steady soothing heartbeat,
What a sight to capture.
It's a gratifying vastness,
Its dreamy surface,
Its dormant strength,
Kind of makes me nervous.
The waves crawl to the shore,
The ebbing tides are peaceful,
Kindling in their own symphony,
Tranquil and blissful.
As the sun scorches my body,
Seagulls squawking over my head,
Horizon stitched with a silver line,
Only serenity I felt.
The sun is laminating with warmth,
The sea slumbering in its blue robe,
A salty smell circulating the air,
Sound is warm and light is soft.
Occasional sounds,
Echo from the cliffs,
This is Heaven's hideaway,
And the greatest gift.
And then I think,
I am like the sea,
For the simple reason that,

No one can control me.
I am like the sea,
You need to dive deep into my depths,
To find the pearls,
And the hidden strength.
I am like a deep sea,
You can only see the shallow part,
With warm shiny water,
But beneath it's dark.

LOOK AT ME

What are you thinking,
When you look at me,
A foolish little girl?
Not very wise,
Who only stutters,
And can't give the right reply?
When you scream loudly,
"I wish you'd try!"
You're not looking at me,
Just open your eyes,
I'll tell you who I am,
As I sit here so still,
As I watch your reactions,
While I explain with thrill,
I am a girl who's nice and free,
I have wings for feet,
Carefree and untroubled,
And my passion bubbled.
Quiet all the time,
Rarely speak my mind,
Might look like a loner,
While sitting in a corner.
But still very curious,
And a passionate dreamer,
After all, a delusional believer.

DRINK

Drink for happiness and become miserable,
Drink for energy and become exhausted,
Drink to forget and start reminiscing,
Drink to have fun and get filled with sorrow,
Drink to socialize and get alienated,
Drink to release stress and become anxious,
Drink to relax and become violent,
Drink to sleep and end up passing out,
Drink like others and become worse than them,
Drink to lose inhibitions and be obnoxious,
Drink the "liquid courage" and start deteriorating,
Drink in control and lose sobriety instead,
Drink only once and become addicted,
Drink to improve mood and get depressed,
Drink because you're curious and become regretful,
Drink to get bold and get crazy,
Drink to be instinctive and lose control,
Drink to start romance and destroy relationships,
Drink for love and get hate,
Drink to sleep and get hungover,
Drink never and be happy forever.

AS A CHILD

Things seem magical,
When you are a child,
Not a care at all,
Open to the world around.
What will occur next,
For them it doesn't matter,
As they have no responsibility,
Over what happens.
You don't make plans,
Or make sure things go as expected,
Not afraid of looking foolish,
When image isn't everything.
They know life is worthy,
Adventure around the corner,
Embedding figments of imagination,
Seeing the world in full color.
Remember that childlike awe,
That used to be your perpetual state,
Just for one moment,
Try to get that back.
Disregard adulthood,
You have an entire life to do that,
Take a break from it,
And in time, go back.

From Soul to Paper – Krisel Qurku

OPTIMISTIC

Outlook determines what our health will become,
Predict a better future, vision as bright as the sun,
The opportunities are in every difficulty,
I'll be willing to show you what this means,
My life is as gratifying as I think it is,
Internal change affects it drastically,
Situations of some sort might try to bring me down,
May I also say, I will quickly get back up.

Intricacies don't have much power over me,
Seeing the glass half full, is a learnable skill.

Things will always work out in the end,
Here I am to help you, my friend,
Everlasting is your joy as things turn out best.

Keep your chin up and you will be fine,
Everyone is certain that you're meant to thrive,
You can now read the first letter of each line.

IN NEED OF A BREAK

I just need a break from being myself,
A break from everything that makes me feel distressed,
A break to let go of all my burdens,
To stop trying to be my best version.

To put an end to these maddening sounds,
That my ears can hardly cope with,
To completely get out of my skin,
Then you'll know that I have lost it.

I want to start showing my genuine self,
The one I don't relate to,
Since everything around me feels delusional,
No one else deserves to feel like this too.

Their words are stabbing like knives in my throat,
Getting on my nerves, fine, you've won,
There's a place where I left my soul,
Far behind, at this point, I don't know.

PAINTED

My mind is an art studio,
That I allow few to explore,
Imagine an enormous white canvas,
Some have attempted,
To leave a mark,
But just made a sketch,
Since the room grew dark.
My blank mind,
Hides immense capability within,
Combined with the courage to speak up,
Put all my rough sketches out there,
Not just throw them in the bin.
I offer some my pencil,
As my eraser wears down,
Speaking with words full of color,
Very witty and smart.
I use my words like a kid with a marker,
Leaving marks all over people,
But I don't let anyone into my studio,
Without them, it's quite peaceful.
I won't allow them to touch my murals,
Or even make the slightest edit,
Because they might manage to impact my life,
And for that, they do not deserve credit.

IMPRESS YOU

What will it take,
To sing a part of your verse,
In the ocean of your thoughts,
I want to immerse.

What will it take,
To be in your pleasant, tense dreams,
To be your "good morning" and "good night",
To live everything I can esteem.

So, tell me, what will it take,
Should I write you a poem, a song,
Should I change who I am,
For you to never do me wrong.

What will it take,
To leave an indelible impression,
Should I become someone else,
Or just try to seek your expression?

WONDERING

I wonder if you're somewhere near,
Or if you're somewhere far,
I wonder if you elicit the memory of me,
Or if we're gazing at the same star.

It's funny how people change,
In the blink of an eye,
You shatter my heart, kill my feelings,
And never care to tell me why.

You were always asking questions,
But never listened to what I said,
Never got to complete a sentence,
But turned your back on me instead.

I asked you for directions,
Which were too complex to follow,
Now I am going in circles,
Looking for a better tomorrow.

But I will never abandon hope,
I know that I must go on,
Starting from tomorrow,
When a new sunrise will be born.

EMPOWERED

Women are unabashedly themselves,
They're stouthearted and unafraid,
They demand their rights and call out wrongs,
In the end, fortune favors the brave.

Feisty and unspoken,
Uninhibited and opinionated,
Boldly passionate,
Openly speaking about being discriminated.

Thanks to them, we are blessed,
They can reform the society,
They play essential role in making headway,
Entrenching principles and morals.

They stand out in many fields,
Nonetheless their triumph stays concealed,
Women contribute significantly,
Therefore, let's all support them unconditionally!

ME AND THE MEADOW

I came across a meadow,
That looked like a page from my storybook,
No, I am not embellishing, dear reader,
But you didn't look at it at the start of autumn as I looked.

Most leaves are hellhound-red in color,
The rest are burnt orange or a vibrant molten gold,
The trees look bare and skeleton-thin,
While leaves, one by one they drop.

Going there at night,
I noticed wind music of the trees,
Impaling mountains come into sight,
I feel dewy air mixed in the breeze.

Me and this meadow have a lot in common,
Way more than you might think,
Although it's dark and murky at first,
It becomes a paradise after you sink in it deep.

SIMPLICITY

What is a simple life?
Is it defined by my needs?
Is it defined by my expectations?
Is it what my heart feeds?
We live in different lifestyles,
And we adapt them to be simple,
Therefore, "simple" is,
For personal interpretation,
You don't need a tiny house,
Or to wear all black,
Or a small cabin nestled,
Alongside a lake.
Quiet and minimal,
Simple living dream,
But not my type of it,
My life is fully examined,
And needs prioritized,
Like never before.
Wanting less is better,
Than having more.

TO MY YOUNGER SELF

Dear younger me,

Here I am sitting on this chair,
Staring at my computer screen,
Content with what I've become,
Reminiscing about who I've been.

It took me years to teach myself happiness,
It took time and discipline to update my brain,
Of course, it will not erase all your trauma,
But I have what is needed to reduce the pain.

I am your future, still hoping to find myself,
Yes, you might be disappointed how you turned out to be,
I still have that list of goals you made,
I'm thrilled to say I have achieved half of these.

Life is beautiful out here,
It's not perfect, but still delightful,
Forgive yourself for being downhearted,
As you'll soon become prudent and insightful.

NIGHT TEARS

Every night as duskiness falls,
She feels the throbbing in her chest,
Trapped between her room's walls,
As she tries to get some rest.

She keeps her tearstained pillow close,
And the pain starts pouring down,
She cries with a heart burned by frost,
Hoping she'll be safe and sound.

You come across her during the day,
And think her life is going well,
But as soon as evening sets,
She is in her own hell.

She knows she won't feel better soon,
The song of sorrow lingers in her ears,
She cries under the midnight moon,
And sheds her bashful tears.

She will tell you her worries,
She believes you do not care,
Because, when she needed help the most,
It's a shame no one was there.

She carefully controls herself,
Not to show what she's feeling inside,
She screams with her hand over her mouth,
It's crazy what a smile can hide.

VALUE OF TIME

Time,
A healer and a killer,
You wonder if you're using it right,
Or will your end be very bitter,
Time sometimes puts and to your problems,
And sometimes it's the problem itself,
It teaches the art of letting go,
Just so you can find yourself.
Time is what we want most,
But also what we use first,
And this waste will have the cost,
Of never being able to satisfy your thirst.
Most of us fail to realize,
The consequences our actions will have,
Thrown into panic,
By the possibility of mistakes.
Time is a precious gift,
Careful who you give some of yours to,
Spend it with the wones who truly love you,
In the end you only regret things we didn't do.
Don't be afraid of slow progress,
Be afraid of standing still,
Do what time does, keep going,
Always willing to take a risk.

WHY WAIT

I finished my assignment,
Two minutes before I heard the bell,
On the day it's due,
Exhausting my brain cells.
I pushed my mental capacity,
Towards the most intense moment,
Four hours I spent in relaxing rest,
Four hours I could have spent on that project.
Although those pleasing moments of peace,
Are not as crucial as my grade,
I'd rather delay until tomorrow,
Than do remarkable work today.
How nerve wrecking is the battle,
Between my two sides,
One, a persistent worker,
The other, very lazy somehow.
I'm sure that many live like this,
And you can choose to change,
Start doing what you've been putting off,
It's high time you mend your ways.
Say "No" to procrastination
Start achieving bit by bit,
Prioritize your tasks,
And nothing will seem too big.

TO MY SPECIAL SOMEONES

Things are never as scary,
When you have a true friend,
Knowing you'll always be supported,
Never fails to bring out your best.

Things might come to an end as we part ways,
But our memories will last forever,
Our sweet adventures refresh my soul,
We either live now or never.

True friends are hard to find,
And even harder to leave,
You've stuck with me in my darkest chapters,
There's no love stronger than the one we give and receive.

I have known you for so long,
I'll treasure both the tears and the laughter,
For us, nothing ever felt wrong,
And in time, our hearts got sharper.

I MISS THE OLD YOU

I miss you,
No, wait,
I miss the old you,
The one who cared,
The one who made me smile,
The one who talked to me every day,
The one who couldn't see me cry.
I miss the old you,
The one who found time for me,
The one I used to talk to,
The one for whom I was a priority.
I look through old photos,
And old messages,
It brings a smile to my face,
And I should not be thinking of it.
But I can't help it,
I can't stop thinking what the past did,
It really meant something to me,
At some point I thought it would have lasted.

SILENCE IS LOVELY

I am quiet,
Tranquil,
Uninterrupted,
And when irritated,
I remain silent.
Quiet mouths,
Are busy minds,
I still get noticed,
Though I don't say much.
It's the quiet ones,
Who draw the most attention,
When there's sound all around,
And a whirlwind of tension,
I am quiet,
Like the eye of the storm,
I find real comfort,
In sitting still,
My soul becomes prudent,
It always will.
Being quiet enough,
And undisturbed enough,
Is a process of discovery,
Leading to recovery.
Talking guides me,
But being quiet protects me,
I absorb knowledge,
From those smarter than me,
And I repel ignorance,
From those more unversed than me,
Never assume that,
Loud is strong,

And quiet is weak,
It can be the complete opposite.
It's insecurities that are loud,
And confidence is silent,
Imagination gets creative,
And in the end,
I'm smiling,
I have been longing,
To stumble upon real silence.
To fill this hollow world,
But such conditions are priceless.

HAUNTING PAST

I've been hurt in the past,
It haunts me in ways I can't describe,
And I have to endure it courageously,
While guilt and fear pound from the inside.

Anger redirects against myself,
And I'm trying with every fiber of my being,
Not to build up walls of defense,
Not to be afraid of feeling.

I have created a fearful future,
Thanks to my frightening past,
Although the past is now history,
In my mind it proceeds to last.

And it's making me collapse,
It burns within my veins,
Pushes me to see these ceaseless scares,
Leaving me stuck in guilt's chains.

My memories can shapeshift,
Sometimes they're faint and soft,
Until they get shrill and alarming,
Dying to hark back to the heartsease I've now lost.

I'm anxious to be drawn against my past,
As it's determined not to recede,
My bond with it is arduous,
And I whimper as I bleed.

From Soul to Paper – Krisel Qurku

I have reached a point where I'm numb to pain,
Something I now scarcely feel,
All this throbbing has driven me insane,
Waiting for my soul to heal.

When the memories come to visit me,
I always sought to escape,
But I'll stop running,
At last I'm wide awake.

I will proudly announce,
That I am willing to let go,
I will allow faith to arise,
And I'll take full control.

I will open up my heart,
Extirpate the roots of pain and hurt,
There I'll plant the seed of hope,
Bury deep the lessons learnt.

CHAPPED LIPS

My lips are chapped and dry,
Maybe it's the coldness outside,
Maybe it's something I ate,
Or could they be irritated by the sun.

Maybe my lips are just tired,
Tired of being sealed for so long,
Damaged my tears that have reached them,
Left wondering if they said something wrong.

My lips are dry,
Blood coming out from between the cracks,
It hurts when I stretch them to smile,
As my heart tries to find the energy it lacks.

Although it hurts when I fake a smile,
My heart is in much more pain,
Its happiness is being drained,
Pumping blood towards the cracks.

Should I try applying some chapstick?
Will they soon be healed,
But I guess I have become used to it,
And the pain is always concealed.

YOU SHOULDN'T HAVE COME

Why?
Why did you come so close?
When you knew you would let me go,
Leaving me filled with woe,
You walked away without warning,
Was this preordained?
Should I have known?
You should have never come into my life,
Never, not at all.
There was no point in letting this happen,
And now you made my spirits dampen,
My mind is sprinting out of control,
As the faded memories start to crawl,
And I'll cry a waterfall,
It's those haunting words I continue to recall.
How did I let myself fall?
When all I remember are those playful strolls,
That I took by myself,
Thinking I was blessed,
But now it's over,
I need to stop and get some rest
From this mental exhaustion,
Until it will cause no harm,
I just want you to know that
You shouldn't have come.

WEEKEND

Saturday morning,
She wakes up broken but with hope,
Her eyes swollen from a sleepless night,
But she's positive that she can cope.

Saturday afternoon,
She's keeping herself busy,
Always afraid to seek help,
and her thoughts make her feel dizzy.

Saturday evening,
She's staying inside,
Cooks herself something tasty,
Says a prayer to feel satisfied.

Saturday night,
She lays numb in bed,
Boosting herself with the strength,
To do it all over again.

Sunday morning,
She feels a gleam of joy,
She has now decided to shine,
In a way that no one can destroy.

Sunday afternoon,
She finds happiness within,
Thrives in a dream like state of mind
Releasing the anguish she always kept in.

Sunday evening,
She's finding solace with her surrounding,
She found reality lulling,
Enough to calm her pounding.

Sunday night,
She's laying in bed reassured and pleased,
About to fall in the arms of a dream,
And from now on she'll believe!

FRAGILE

I want to treat everyone like they're
Fragile,
Delicate,
Breakable,
Damaged,
Hence, I don't hurt the ones who actually are.
For I know that I, myself have been hurt,
When I was fragile,
Delicate,
Breakable,
Damaged.
You'll never know who is easily hurt,
The fragile ones wear thick layers of armor,
And put on a brave face,
To conceal a heart made of glass,
Unable to resolve the burning sadness.
And so, they come off as strong,
But refuse to form any bond,
And if this armor is touched,
You'll see the tears that hide,
And these tears created rust.
They will build up shields,
To protect parts they're not willing to share,
And if they decide to open up to you,
Please, handle with care.

SOCIETY AND THE GIRL

Hello, I am society,
Look what a pretty girl you are,
I'll help you become your "best version"
From now on, we'll never be apart.

I'll give you rules, limits, judgements,
But they're just to keep you safe,
You should live up to my expectations,
But don't complain about feeling fake.

I want to see flawless, shiny skin,
I'll show you examples from magazines,
You'll become more self-conscious,
When you'll become a teen.

Love your body, but not too much,
And take care of that extra weight,
No matter what, cover up your body,
It's the boys you shouldn't distract.

If I don't accept your shape,
Then go on a drastic diet,
Or even starve yourself,
Make your stomach keep quiet.

Keep in mind, your grades define you,
And everyone will comment on your results,
I'll make you study in a field that you don't like,
But at least you'll be known as a responsible adult.

From Soul to Paper – Krisel Qurku

You'd look pretty in that dress,
And wear heels you need to look tall,
A bit of makeup here and there,
You look pretty after all.

You want to fall in love,
I'll tell you who and when,
You'll be safe from judgement,
Only if I craft your taste in men.

Did someone harass you?
And you want to stand up for yourself?
It's not ladylike to raise your voice,
So just sit down and accept your fate.

I wonder why you cry at night,
Depression is not what you feel,
You are simply exaggerating,
And you're too young to say such things.

You have a lively fire in you,
I'm afraid it's my job to put it out,
Your ideas are too insane to be heard,
So please, suppress the untamed world you hide.

SOCIETY AND THE BOY

Hello, I am society,
Look what a handsome man you've grown into,
You have to fit a certain gender mold,
And fulfill some stereotypes too.

Tough and physical are what you need to be,
Here you have some magazines as an example,
Make sure you are powerful and in control,
Don't say it's too much to handle.

Everywhere you look, violence is depicted,
And that's how you should be asserting manhood,
That is one way to show your masculinity,
This authority will do you good.

Strive hard to be strong and aggressive,
Your body represents your power and dominance,
You'll be obligated to overcome some challenges,
Don't worry about showing greed and ignorance.

You'll find yourself making decisions on alcohol and drugs,
It's not good for your health, but other boys might call you weak,
Your friends will endlessly pressure you,
These secrets will ruin your family, as you won't be able to speak.

That same pressure will haunt you when you're talking to a girl,
It takes real courage and bravery to tell her how you feel,
But be careful falling for someone,
For the sake of your reputation, vulnerability should be concealed.

From Soul to Paper – Krisel Qurku

You're cool if you're impervious to academic performance,
At the same time, you'll be overwhelmed by expectations,
Which you will find hard to meet,
So, you give up altogether.

You might find all these challenges overwhelming,
I'm not surprised how conflicted you are,
You'll be shielding yourself from criticism,
But I say it's a part of growing up.

The pressure I'll give you is fierce,
But I especially adore patriarchy,
So, hurry up in your process of "manning up"
Though it might seem like an anarchy.

No, you are not allowed to cry,
Boys should never show fragility,
You represent dominance and strength,
For now, hide your sensibility.

I'll be an irreplaceable part of your journey,
And I know what is best for you,
Adjust to my orders well,
Until they no longer feel new.

LET'S DISAPPEAR

Let's disappear,
Like the moon on a darkest night,
Leaving behind bright or vague stars,
Or a thick magical darkness covering the night.

Let's fade away,
Like the sun going down leaving behind swirls of colors,
Sure that it will still glow the next day,
And letting the gloominess take over.

Let's fade away into the mist,
And get lost within ourselves,
Ignore the miserable valleys and troughs,
And not let anything get in our way.

Let's vanish completely,
Melt into nothingness, until time doesn't stride,
To be overlooked upon by lands and oceans,
And become entirely dry.

EVEN IF

Even if my heart was taken away,
You'd still be the one I loved.

Even if my eyes were blinded,
You'd still be the only one I saw.

Even if my hands where shortened,
You'd still be the one for whom I wrote.

Even if my brain was pulled to pieces,
You'd still be in my thoughts.

Even if my ears were deafened,
It wouldn't be a shame,
I'd still hear everyone who mentioned your name.

But even if I died at this very moment,
My soul would still suffer for you,
All of these I would have gone through,
If I knew you felt what I feel too.

SIPPING

I am sipping on my tea,
Hoping the herbs will cleanse my rotting soul,
And enhance my heart's wellness,
Since it's been raging without control.

But there's one significant issue,
Although it will strongly cleanse my body,
Do away with the harm, toxicity, and crush the rustiness,
But this is not what I wish upon me,
I want it to do away with the foul decomposing sorrow,
And replace it with flourishing loveliness.

This drink is strong enough to hug my desolate spirit,
To make me forget my heartache, my ego, my regret and misery,
Always hopeful, I'll keep on sipping…

FIREFLIES

They are the stars dancing in the night,
Showing off their blinking sparkle,
Lightening themselves up,
Specks of playful lights, so artful.

These tiny shiny creatures,
Find the darkest corners,
And fill it a glimmer of light,
Whispering "hope" to the night crawlers.

They are proof that magic is around,
On eerie nights they glow,
Speaking with their enchanting flame,
A language we will never know.

These dimes of brightness among the trees,
That I watch radiantly as they flicker,
And they softly sit on my hand,
Like dreams, they both vanish and shimmer.

A NOTE TO YOU

This note is for you,
Who smiles through the pain,
Though you are in vain,
Who go through everyday tasks,
Even when you can't.

This note is for you,
When you're going through a challenge,
While spreading hope as much as you can manage,
For you are strong enough,
And you can deal with the damage.

This note is for you,
Who acknowledges yourself,
Never compared to someone else,
You know you're worthy and absolute,
A creature full of grace.

FERVENT SUN

Golden, hot, dazzling sun,
Let me be enchanted by your majestic beauty,
For you bring life to our sacred nature,
And make your marvelous rays pursue me.

You fill our souls with warmth,
Exiting a gleam of motivation,
Until my skin feels notably scorched,
I'm impacted by this fierce vibration.

And once you fall to an end,
You'll still be gracefully reborn,
Teaching me love and peace in the morning,
Like a sunshine kiss at the crack of dawn.

So dear sacred, triumphant sun,
Shower your luminous rays upon me,
Give me fearlessness and your passion,
Envision a future just as bright beyond me.

DON'T BE AFRAID

Don't be afraid to say "I'm sorry",
No more wasting time on regrets and worries.

Don't be afraid to say "I messed up",
You're imperfectly worthy, don't say you're not enough.

Don't be afraid to say "I'm trying",
You'll make it through all the sweat and tears from crying.

Don't be afraid to say "I am not fine",
Soon after the pain, your will shine.

Don't be afraid to say "I need help",
Soon enough, you won't regret taking that step.

Don't be afraid to say "No!",
Own up to yourself, make your dignity known.

Don't be afraid to say "I love you",
And enjoy the tremble of the passionate sky above you.

HOW DO I PUT IT

How do I put into words,
Your pure, youthful beauty,
Your soulful brown eyes,
Which look right through me,
Radiating your genuine happiness,
That look is special truly.
And your bright sensitive lips,
Whose smile cheers me up absolutely,
With every word you say, I am amazed,
This is how I gaze at your amiable face.
And when your strong, welcoming arms,
Are ready to pull me in a hug,
And listen to your heart,
Such a subtle charm.
Your skin is always glowing,
Reflects the euphoria bursting from within,
Your body full of genial warmth,
You are the source where my passion begins.

THE SUNSET

I've never seen such a magnificent sunset,
And maybe I'll never see a sunset that's sweeter,
I hastily ran to catch it,
But it crouched even deeper.

I screamed "Please don't go!"
Like I had never told anyone before,
I said "Please stay with me!"
But it never stopped.

I asked "Please stay near me!"
I begged while bursting into tears,
For the first time in my life,
There was something I would miss.

I am deeply sorry, my pride,
For the first time I apologize,
I am sorry I brought myself down,
In front of a setting sun.

LOVE, I SHOULD LET YOU GO

Love, I should let you go,
Trust me, it's not a simple task to accomplish,
But because of you, my life was demolished,
But please, don't hate me, for I still love you…
But when the mind listened to the heart,
It was hard for me to get through,
I know you still love,
I know because I know you,
You can leave,
And still come back if you want to.
But even if I love,
I won't wait for you, trust me…
You think it's easy, this haunting pain?
Of us being so close yet so separated,
Which is why love is something I should be forgetting.
I can't bear with your heart wearing the mask of hatred,
Which only deceived and made things complicated.
But I won't be leaving forever,
No, no…my heart still loves,
I'll return again, once I recover,
I know it will be too late,
You see, when I see you, I still shudder,
And your hand will be stroking another,
But don't be afraid,
I will not suffer,
It's enough to see her heart cherish yours,
And fill it to the brim with warmth
Well then, love, I should let you go…

SHE

She was an ordinary girl,
But there was no other girl alike,
She was resilient and strong,
She never complained or cried.

That's simply how she is,
Or to be correct, she was,
She lost all she ever had,
And now all she sees is flaws.

She forgot the sparkling stars,
That she playfully gazed at every night,
She forgot all the joyous smiles,
Tears now blind her sight.

She got lost,
She's awake only in nothingness
She faded into the mountains,
The mournful wind carries her numbness.

MEMORY LANE

You often go for a walk down the memory lane,
To relive some precious moments you've experienced,
To see how you would address a situation now that you've changed,
To go back to the loss that is making you feel delirious.

Maybe you take a trip down the memory lane,
Because you know you will bump into someone who is special,
And it will be at a time when it all felt normal,
Why is it amusing to feel nostalgic and sentimental?

Probably because a memory, is also a treasure,
These invaluable treasures, they make you smile,
Cherished reminisces can also be painful,
Knowing you'll never regain those times so worthwhile.

Going back in time but with a current mindset,
Might make your sanity slip through the cracks of your mind,
To relive the same experience that shaped what you are,
To be unwilling to leave the past behind.

Though I don't blame you, your past created your identity,
With hindsight you realize what was and wasn't right,
The range of emotions you've endured,
Makes you fully understand how everything will be alright.

LIES WE SAY

"How are you? Well, I'm fine."
"It's true, I'm doing great."
"No, I'm not crying, something's in my eye."
"What makes you think I'm lonely or desolate."
"I'm confident. I don't need any help."
"No matter what they say about me, I simply don't care."
"I'll support whatever you choose."
"I'm sure it's something I can bear."
"You are doing a great job."
"I am very happy to see you."
"I would be nothing without you."
"What I feel is that I love you."
"Everyone is perfect except for me."
"Look at me, I am so ugly."
"I should soon start to change."
"Something is definitely wrong with my body."
"I am not worthy of love."
"I don't deserve to live."
"It would be okay without me."
"I have nothing to offer here."
"I am not lying, it's the truth."
"I would never do that to you."
"I'm not hurt, I'm over it."
Please, stop lying, I can still see right through you.

LESSON LEARNED

I've loved, lost, and failed,
But most of all, I've learned,
Through darkness and difficult times,
Wisdom and experience are earned.

I've learned how to always be grateful,
Even when I'm unhappy or miserable,
Despite all the distress that's taken over my mind,
A glimmer of delight must be made visible.

I've learned to stay calm,
To make myself comfortable with everything,
Enhance inner strength and faith,
And praise the value that patience brings.

It's a shame we aren't taught such things,
Only from experience, after we've been hurt and bruised,
The past is where these lessons were received,
And the present and future is when they are used.

YOU NEED YOU

Take a moment, a deep breath,
Lay down and focus on yourself,
Notice what might concern your health,
Let all your cells relax.

Notice how something's not right,
Your shoulders ache, your limbs feel tight,
Even if the discomfort is slight,
Pain comes to your sight.

Notice how your own body is calling for help,
Yet, you tend to overlook yourself,
This worrying concern withheld,
Given you want to take care of someone else.

Put yourself first,
Your own matters deserve attention,
Stop pulling yourself to pieces for others,
Be your own intervention.

HEAVEN ON EARTH

I can swear,
There is no heaven that I haven't felt with you,
In the embrace of your affectionate arms,
While showing off your charm,
Setting off these startling yet reassuring alarms,
That keep ringing in my head,
With every closer step you take,
I believe that's the heaven I felt.
I saw angels in your mind and heart,
Decisions being heartfelt, not smart,
But resisting those alluring eyes is hard.
They overpower me,
Longing to devour the deepest, hidden parts of my being,
And if heaven isn't what I'm feeling,
You'll always be the paradise that I'll be seeking.
And if heaven is not
The uplifting peace,
The innocent bliss,
Or the boundless devotion that you give,
Then I don't want any of it.

AFRAID OF BEING AFRAID

Don't we all get overwhelmed by the feeling of utter fear,
Crippling from under your skin.
But isn't fear what we really should be afraid of?
So frightening with its shadow so big.

Fear has instilled a false illusion,
That everything is worse than it seems,
It leads into emotions like anger and hate,
All of them fake and none of it real.

Fear is a state of mind,
Putting us in a stressful trance,
Pushing us into a frenzy,
Makes us forget to seek any chance.

But fear, is the only barrier holding us back,
From taking the leap of faith leading to happiness,
This why fear is what we should fear,
Convincing us we're safer in enclosed emptiness.

Fear is what set the boundaries that have blocked feeling,
The fear of fear is why we should venture into the unknown,
And if fear isn't scary enough, regret should be,
Free your mind and break your heart of stone.

GUILTY PLEASURE

Is it sin or virtue,
Am I happy or ashamed,
For what gives you pleasure,
You must not be blamed.

Why should we pay a price,
For doing what makes us happy,
Why make a fuss out of it,
Or doubt yourself if you're ready.

This can be a simpler concept,
Where guilty pleasure does not exist,
The same goes to feelings like guilt or regret,
If we crave something, we must chase it.

No matter how little the joy lasts,
Sometimes, it's worth the risk,
Some chances can make us come alive,
And these chances don't leave time to think.

Life is messy, even in the comfort zone,
And boundaries can't always leave people out,
Life should be enjoyed as it is,
So, grab the opportunity when it comes!

ONCE AGAIN

They come once again,
At a time where your heart has cleansed itself,
Of all the feelings,
But they come once again,
With the sweetest greetings,
And worst of all,
You find it appealing,
You find yourself smiling though you shouldn't,
You're confused,
You're left wondering,
Whether you should risk your heart already bruised,
If what hurt you can heal your wound,
Should you let yourself be fooled,
By this ever-surprising kindness,
That never fails to capture your attention,
To the point it becomes your intervention,
But what is important to remember,
Is that some things are doomed to fail,
But that's not always the case,
After all,
Don't we all deserve a second chance?
To prove that we can change,
And that we can learn from mistakes,
While improving ourselves.
For sure,
Unlike the first try, you are ready for the second,
You know what's coming towards you,
You don't overlook the red flags before you,
And this is where you realize,
How hard it is to come by forgiveness,
And acceptance of the situation you are in,

From Soul to Paper – Krisel Qurku

But remember how strong you are within,
It takes strength to risk it all once again,
Even after all the dishonor and mistrust that was left,
You convinced yourself that it will all turn out great,
Not many have this power and fearlessness,
Thus, take pride in that.
Forgiveness is growth,
And if you are the one who messed up,
But you're still treated with a kind approach,
Consider yourself lucky,
That you're given the opportunity to retry,
But don't be surprised if you're met with withdrawal,
Some can't get over the tears they've cried,
Or the regret they have to hide,
It will be a long journey,
To win credibility once again,
As time goes by,
This chance is not something you should disregard,
Put back together the pieces of their heart,
Prove to be what you first promised,
Not only to others, to yourself too,
Yes, it hurts to be faced with the truth,
And to adapt to a situation that is new,
But this time it's not new anymore,
You now know how to rise back after a fall,
The initial bitterness won't last for long,
If you don't repeat doing someone wrong.

CRYING COULDS

I stared into the grey dreary sky,
Where the heave clouds want to cry,
To cope with it, they need to let it go.

And what makes the cloud feel bad,
Is that people start feeling sad,
When its tears knock on the window.

And people hide, start running inside,
While the cloud slowly dies,
Until it can't rain anymore.

Sometimes, the clouds have company,
And it's sad to witness somebody,
In a corner, crying alone.

For some the rain is music,
That prevents them from losing it,
Forgetting what they've undergone,

Either way, I find solace in this weather,
After rain there's rainbow, it will get better,
The magic inside every single drop.

A PRINCESS

Darling, you are a princess,
You possess strength and power,
Which make you brave, even when weak,
Upon anything you might encounter.

Your birth was your coronation,
Your sweetness comes along the way,
Your confidence is exemplary,
You respect, you don't obey.

You don't need a savior or a prince,
Be your own knight in shining armor,
Set yourself free, rise on your own,
Even if everything gets harder.

So princess, it's high time you fix your crown,
With or without a prince by your side,
Make your good intentions clear,
Let your faith flourish inside.

CHANGE LIKE THE SEASONS

I awaken like the breeze of spring,
And bloom like its flowers,
Entertains the playful chirps,
Of a bird at an early hour.

I crash down like the waves of the summer sea,
And cool off like the light summer breeze,
Be the sunshine that warms your soul,
And whisper sweetly like the leaves of exotic trees.

I might shine like the gold that autumn holds,
I can fall at rock bottom like the parched leaves,
Let you admire the gorgeous sunsets,
While enjoying the sound of the leaves' crisp.

And later drown in mellow sadness,
The same way winter creeps in,
While the frigid mornings awaken the consciousness,
Anticipating the turn of spring.

WORDS,

Elegantly combined letters,
To make possible a message,
A brief remark,
To touch someone's soul,
In a unique way that cannot be explained,
How knitted sounds can cause pain,
Or make someone feel drained,
Of their own self.
Sometimes they bring euphoria,
Bliss,
Joy,
To the ear that hears them,
And to the lips that pronounce them,
While silent ones still looking for euphoria,
Bliss,
Joy,
Find them in words in ink,
Pleasant for the eye and not the ear,
Yet words can be so light,
For the wind to swipe easily,
They fade and lose their worth,
To be forgotten and never unearthed.

ATTRACTION

The most attractive thing,
Happens when beauty isn't what attracts,
When importance is placed upon the mind,
The beautiful complexity of thoughts and intellect.

Physical attraction is common,
Spiritual attraction is rare,
It's hard to resist someone who gives you butterflies,
Not in your stomach but in your head.

Perfection is admirable,
But have you seen the rawness in someone wild,
It's the liveliness in vulnerability,
Only visible once you let down your guard.

Attraction comes and goes,
But love will stay,
And if it doesn't,
It was never meant to be that way.

I see no reason behind short-lived passion,
Be attracted to the one who will be devoted to you,
Want the best for yourself,
To attract the one who wants the best for you.

DANCE

Dance under the moonlit night,
Dance until the death of love.

Dance until you alter the rhythm of your heart,
Dance with the one with whom you'll never be apart.

Dance in the way your soul wants you to dance,
Dance carelessly without making a plan.

Dance with someone who'll hold you right,
Dance for the feelings that you can't fight.

Dance like the night will not be stopping,
Dance like you do when no one is watching.

Dance to your heart's content,
Make it the might you'll never forget.

GHOST

Today I felt as if,
I was followed by a ghost,
An uneasy presence,
Not letting me go,
At any cost.

I recognize this feeling,
It's haunted me before,
But it was better,
Back when I had what I lost.

It's the leftover feelings,
That won't go away,
As much as I hate them,
I want them to stay.

WITHIN

The thoughts linger lasciviously in the mind,
The body slithers to their kind,
The heavenly union two becoming one,
Fulfilling what's been left undone.

Romanticism in the form of stardust,
Spurting from every pore of one's skin,
Auras colliding into blazing passion,
Dangerously merging into the naught of sin.

Sweltering strokes make muscles flinch,
Hand grasping, greedy for the unity to continue,
Heavy, fragrant breaths imperfectly synchronized,
Heartily pounding away any issue.

Eyes filled with hunger, blinded by flashing lights,
Two entities magnetized towards one,
Surrendered bodies to the control of adoration,
The place to escape to, unable to run.

Golden treasure dripping as spiraling galaxies,
Eternity in one smile, in one cry,
Untamed mirages lit up from underneath,
Shrieking as more time goes by.

Loving until one becomes a stranger to oneself,
The maze of one tangled in the valley of the other,
Touches etched into intrepid souls,
Which have yet to uncover.

INK

I was thinking about getting a tattoo,
Then I look at my reflection on the mirror,
And realize my body is already covered,
In permanent meaningful markings,
That have recently become clearer,
And its strong messages that they deliver.
Skin darker here, but glowing there,
Burning places touched by your hand,
Scars made by distressing accidents,
Tanned beauty by sun's best intents.
My body's covered in invisible ink,
Ink made of joy and pain,
Even etched in memories,
Made of what I most regret,
There is no tattoo that can outweigh,
The value of what has already been written,
Nor rewrite a story,
That can change what's given.

A BIT OF LIFE, A BIT OF LOVE

A bit of life is what I needed,
A little love is what I craved,
But all I got was emptiness,
Unnecessary blank space.

A little courage to lift me up,
Instead of burdensome disappointment,
To tune me in with the despair,
To make everything seem pointless.

Little did I know,
I had all the inspiration in me,
Only I could heal myself,
As long as I believed.

In the continuity of time,
I'll continue to try hard,
There's always a way out,
With a little life, a little love.

THE PERSON READING THIS

The person reading this,
Is stuck in a rut,
Trying to comprehend how the world works,
And know which strings to tug.

The person reading this is confused,
Dying to know what they think or feel,
To make sense of their perplexed thoughts,
Locate the numb ones they want to kill.

The person reading this needs affection,
Give up their act of being unbothered,
And showing they're human and in need of care,
To seek healing after what they've suffered.

The person reading this is reassured and filled with faith
The kind of faith you can't easily shake
They acknowledge they'll receive what's best
To not live a life full of regret.

BREAK FREE

At this very moment, right now,
I put a tempting offer out,
One to unleash your inner blissful self,
To emphasize the favorite traits of yourself.

To get yourself out of a cage you're locked in,
Like an a wild animal tamed to comfort,
One satisfied with what they have,
Who never put itself first.

I'm handing you the keys to this cage,
Sure, it will be hard out there,
But you can experience much more,
Than what you then already had.

You freeze, you, stutter,
You're satisfied with what you have,
In the comfort zone of having just enough,
You acknowledge yet accept being trapped.

You're adapted to this type of living,
Understood, you're quite satisfied,
But what stories will you tell your grandchildren,
At the old age of sixty-five?

That story about being late to work,
Or missing an event since you were working long hours,
What about how you managed being underpaid,
Will you tell about your boss and those dreadful encounters?

How about the story where you rose from the bottom,
Became a living version of your happiest dreams,
Describe the hardships of rags to riches,
And going to some great extremes?

Reflect on the above-mentioned statements,
I think my points are made clear by now,
Make a plan, write things down,
Now's the time to actively visualize.

SOULMATES

I believe in soulmates,
I believe there is one person ideally fit for someone,
A person with whom the connection is strong from the beginning,
The one to make the mind go spinning,
And the lips continuously grinning,
And a whole hour feels like a minute.
Can I scientifically prove the existence of soulmates?
No, I'm unable to prove it,
For science focuses on time and distance,
Things which true bonds ignore,
Instead, they beg with insistence,
To always have their affection and assistance,
Face the peace that was not present before.
This person will be your guide,
They will show you who you really are,
Reveal your deepest secrets and scars,
Make effort to heal them over time,
And strip you off your ego,
Process that can be addicting and slow,
It's a magical miracle,
Makes you feel desperate and vulnerable,
To this state of being so pure and safe,
Which you don't want to let go,
This emotional vulnerability will chafe,
Your happiness is what they'll aim,
Open your eyes wide awake,
For all negativity to be drained,
In one short embrace,
Your heart shattered to pieces,
Will be flowed with tenderness through the cracks,
And stuck back together in a snap.

That is what a soulmate can do,
And you'll be doing the same for them.

This bond will go both ways,
To make inner peace stem,
All other worries will be condemned,
Since nothing will matter more,
Than the companionship with them.

WRITE

We don't write to romanticize,
Or to beautify pain and heartbreak,
For it's equal to partial death,
While living through the ache.

We write to empathize with ourselves,
To purge our misery,
To drag up our spirits from hidden depths,
Until misfortune becomes history.

It is not pleasant to live this way,
Nor is it gratifying,
But it has become a coping mechanism,
A crucial means of surviving.

DREAM

To dream is not a waste of time,
Dreams are upcoming realities,
Planted seeds of the future,
Made of genuine fantasies,
I will never cease to dream,
I will only stop dreaming,
When sky meets earth,
When sun meets moon,
When the sun comes up at night,
When the moon comes up at day,
When mirages are real,
When heaven meets hell,
When angels become demons,
When I stop breathing,
That's when I'll stop dreaming,
For right now it's the passion that keeps me alive,
One life is all we have,
So why aren't we running,
Like we've caught fire,
Towards realizing our dreams,
Filled with hope and desire.

FOREVER

Are forevers real,
I have read stories,
About people's glories,
And I have read proses and poetries,
That try to interpret forevers,
Promises kept throughout eternity,
That are never thrown off the deep end,
Commitment that never descends,
How possible is that,
I've heard couples claim real love is forever,
Through every fight and obstacle,
Endlessly, over and over,
Until all is nothingness,
And will stop when they reach infinity.
Yet we may or may not feel,
That forever isn't real,
What about all those fake promises,
And those lost loves,
They're the reasons why I'm suspicious,
Of the deceits of eternity,
Which in itself remains a complex matter.

RAINBOW OF TORMENT

Red was the blood rushing to your wound,
Orange were the leaves you were stepping on,
Yellow was your pale exhausted face,
Green were the stains on your jeans,
Blue were your dry lips unable to speak,
Indigo was the night sky the night I saw you,
Violet were the bruises, the ones around your neck.

I'M SORRY, NO

Unreciprocated love is a popular topic,
Being left begging and longing,
But what some people don't comprehend,
Is what it feels like to be on the other end.

Never being able to understand what they see in you,
Why they feel this way,
Not realizing the depth of their fondness,
Or what you could have changed.

It hurts,
Knowing you've fed the monster called fear or self-doubt,
Yet knowing in your heart, feelings will never sprout.

It's hard when realization hits you,
That no matter how you behave,
What they feel won't wash away.

So, we fall into a distant, reserved friendship,
Knowing it will hurt you, at least for now,
I just wish you could understand,
The fact that I'm suffering a fallout.

I mutter "I'm sorry",
For guilt will always eat me up at night,
Wondering if I did them wrong or right.

I want to end thing on a good note,
But a plain "No" simply isn't in my vocabulary,
I sugarcoat rejection,
Excuses so unnecessary.

You cannot be forced to love,
Or to unlove someone,
Fear and uncertainty are brutal,
Unsure what will become.

I hope you move on,
And remember me as the one who cared,
Maybe your ashtray will be full,
Until you hear from me again,
but keep hoping for the future,
Because love shouldn't make you scared.

WORDS SUPPRESSED

I clearly recall,
The day we first met,
Those uncanny circumstances,
First words we exchanged,
That smile that still haunts me,
And emotions I'd never before felt,
And I'm sure you understood,
What I also didn't express,
Your laugh was no joke,
And so, I winked back,
From that moment I knew,
The feeling was there to stay,
As every word of yours made me sway,
I found myself anticipating these moments,
Yet some messages that I couldn't convey,
Some instincts that I couldn't obey,
Still trouble me to this day,
If only I was able to say,
How your smile makes me sway,
But it was much more than that.
For you, I'd bleed myself dry,
Let blood stream out of my every pore,
Carve out my heart and put it at your feet,
To me this all sounds so bittersweet,
Though to you, it seems deceit,
But you can't push me away,
I'm only going one way,
For you I'd ruin what I am,
And do it all over again.

BED

My bed,
Keeper of secrets, catcher of tears,
Bearer of pain, throughout the years,
Sea of blankets, where emotion flows,
As the night begins to close,
Covers so protective, withholds life's woes,
Keeps them so tightly that no one ever knows,
Collector of dreams, hopes, and fantasies,
Creator of new alternative realities,
Stimulator of thought and reflection,
To break down the choice of a right direction,
It handles quite well the troubles of my heart,
Being so weak and beating itself up,
I scream into my pillow yet it never complains,
It soaks the aches and never goes astray,
When the night has fallen and I'm fast asleep,
It is familiar with the fact that my anxiety will creep.

My bed is always listening,
And though virtues it's got plenty,
There's one thing that's missing,
It is half empty.

BEAUTY, WHERE IS IT?

The human soul yearns for beauty,
Searches for it everywhere,
In art, people, buildings, places, landscapes, love, religion and life,
But what the human soul doesn't know,
Is that beauty is not to be searched for,
It's hungry for something that's good,
Merely because it exists,
It's everywhere; in ourselves, our homes, our soul.

But what about a broken soul,
I'd say it still flourishes in its own uniqueness,
For a broken soul is beauty shattered in pieces,
The more it screams, the more a crack increases,
While it does it leaves room for something else,
Fresher, prettier, way more pleasing,
But what's really messing with my reasoning,
Is why human mind can't come to terms,
With such replacement.

If we were really born in a world,
Where learning has become so broad,
Why is human power so limited,
Why can't we awaken once we fall?
Though we seize every moment,
Every strain of emotion, caught in the stream of life,
Yet still too scared to look behind the curtain,
That hides the infinite unknown to us.

BRIGHT SIDE

I want nothing from the world,
It doesn't owe me a thing,
I just want to exist,
And for the world to acknowledge my existence,
I want to live,
Untamed,
Shameless in what I do,
Embrace the world's wilderness,
I want the sun to teach me its warmth,
I want the wind to teach me its wisdom,
I want the sea to teach me its calmness,
I want the soil to teach me its richness.
The beauty of nature was tailor made for me,
Sky above me, earth below me, and fire within,
Submerged in it, heart and mind,
Embodying a heaven that's hard to find.

LOVE

They say if you love something,
You let it go.

If it returns,
It's forever yours.

And now I am free,
But I look back.

In the distance,
It's always you there.

And if you come back,
I promise I will fight.

To keep you giving meaning,
To my empty life.

I'LL HEAL YOU

To the person I am today...

I'm sorry I've forgotten,
What it feels to be proud of you,
To accept your faults,
To cherish your body and soul.

I've told you're not worthy,
That you should hide,
Sorry it took me long to realize,
Your whole being is divine.

I will build you back,
Set you wondrously free,
I'll make you recognize yourself once more,
I promise, I will.

TENSION

When everything's frustrating,
All I hear is screams,
A deadly mixture of anger and irony,
Wish it could disappear by all means.

What is a safe place,
When all that exists is fright,
Maybe I did deserve,
To not grow up so bright.

I'm not a fan of escaping,
From hardships that appear,
But all we can do is remain strong,
Savor the freedom that is near.

Because once we get away,
And left on our own hands,
We'll ease our own sorrow,
In the chapter that will commence.

I don't know where we go from here,
There's so much we might lose,
In an instant, we'll take charge,
That's an option we will choose.

MOONLIT EVENING

Under the starlit sky,
With a bottle of wine,
Washed by the moonlight,
And nonsense in my mind
No friends at hand, no one at all,
Therefore, I poured alone,
I hate loneliness,
So I turned to the brightest star,
Standing out in the sky,
And then I turned to my shadow
That was falling behind.
And so from one, we became three,
Cooled down by the sea breeze,
Until I sipped some more wine,
And posed a question to the star,
"how come, after all this time,
You haven't died, you're more than alive"
It quietly replied,
"Unless you love through the storms,
There's no easy way to survive"
My shadow whispered,
"Take his advice if you really
Want to shine that bright"
I kept emptying glasses,
Until wine started to taste bitter,
But I didn't care,
I liked the dizziness, the numbness,
And I had little joy to spare,
But that night I learned to accept,
That nothing is fair,
Neither the fact that I'm alone,

From Soul to Paper – Krisel Qurku

Nor the fact that the bottle's empty,
But if I don't get disappointed,
There's no way I will get happy.
Though everything I love is long gone,
I will fight this treacherous world alone,
While the greedy are living in luxury,
Swimming in goods taken for granted,
I guess I'll fight for simplicity,
In what's truly enchanting.

OVERWHELMED

She feels too much,
Exceeds her own perception,
"Does anybody care?"
It's her only question.

She longs for the love,
She fails to see in herself,
And ends up getting hurt,
More than anyone else.

She screams to the mirror,
"Is anyone there?"
"Am I on my own?"
"This life can't be fair!"

No one's seen what she's seen,
No one's cried the tears she's cried,
Yet she's still able to unleash faith,
With which she prays every night.

She wants love,
But there's no one to get it from,
She wants trust,
But is willing to give away none.

Everyone respects her,
Admires her being as a whole,
But it's worthless,
If she doesn't understand it though.

From Soul to Paper – Krisel Qurku

If only she knew how special,
And important she was to him,
Maybe things wouldn't be this way,
But her eyes are blinded by fear.

Now she's stressed out, depressed,
Her heart locked away,
Looks up to the sky,
And hopes for better days.

Maybe this state isn't everlasting,
Maybe his feelings are the key,
To a cherished future free of hurt,
Bliss to follow her for eternity.

LOST

I believe when something is lost,
Life has a way of making it,
Come back to us,
Though sometimes,
In the most unpredictable ways,
They're there for us,

The universe has quite a sharp sense of humor,
Because once I stop the search for something,
It's going to appear in front of my eyes,
Once forgotten,
It will keep crossing my mind.

But why when I willingly let you go,
Does the universe disagree,
Is it trying to mess with my mind,
Or is this really meant to be?

POLLUTED LIFE

If all cars were trees,
If airplanes were stars,
If trains were rivers,
We'd be healthier so far.

But fuel isn't sap,
Smog does not show greenery,
Rubbish does not depict flowers,
In sights difficult imagining.

Animals are disappearing,
Nature is losing itself,
But God forbid I speak against it,
When more pressing matters need care.

Global warming is not just an expensive hoax,
Climate change should not be overlooked,
Yet all we care about is technology and media,
But the mind of politics is already booked.

I apologize in advance to future generations,
On behalf of everyone else,
I'm sorry for the agony we've caused,
You truly deserved the best.

THE ANTICIPATED FUTURE

Upon entering adulthood in a few months,
I'll be alone somewhere far,
Not knowing anyone to talk to,
Surrounded by things foreign.

The future seems near,
I'm visualizing glimpses of tomorrow,
But I don't know which path to follow,
And more confusion is taking over.

All people I've encountered,
All friendships I have formed,
When we meet again someday,
Will I recognize them anymore?

I don't have a clue,
Where I'll go from here,
But whichever path I choose,
I'll make success appear.

WISH I WAS…

I wish I was your pillow
So you could lay your head on me,
Pour on your emotions,
And I'd happily drain your tears,

I wish I was your mirror,
So I could look at you every day,
So you would smile at me,
The way you smile to yourself.

I wish I was your phone,
So I could hold your hand,
So you'd tell me everything,
Just like you keep your life in there.

And if I was your bed,
I'd let you curl up in my blankets,
Provide you with my warmth,
And comfort that you're lacking.

MY GENERATION

We are the powerful generation,
That has been withholding immense strength,
Struggled to fill the absence of diversity,
But were silenced along the way.

The silence brought nothing but pain,
Fought back to mental illnesses each day,
Depression, anxiety and disorders,
While no one seemed to care.

We buried our hopes and dreams,
We were forced to do the "right" thing,
But the right thing was a detriment to us,
Thus, it's our right to protest and make a fuss.

While no one's watching over this youth,
That they've poisoned to the core,
Anger still runs deep in our veins,
And we'll stand up to being ignored.

Just look around at the reality we're in,
Where girls are used and boys ashamed,
"My body, my choice" but that doesn't sink in,
As if we were expected to succumb to being tamed.

We're powerful if we're together,
Won't be our choice to surrender,
Bury us deep into the ground,
Just to see us blossom again with splendor.

From Soul to Paper – Krisel Qurku

If we could praise one another,
And help ourselves grow,
Instead of bringing each other down,
We'd scream in a unanimous voice.

I'm certain you see a pattern,
On what I've said above,
Gen Z will revolutionize humanity,
In history we'll go down!

SUGAR

You claim you're so delicious,
Soft like buttercream,
I'm the chocolate flavored cake,
And you're the frosting on top of me.

Your kisses are your sprinkles,
Colorful and playful,
My favorite gingerbread man,
Nicely sweet and tasteful.

I crave for your sugar,
Long for it until my being bleeds,
Dribbles of hot marmalade,
But will you bite into what feeds.

As lips tremble to form words,
I'll be fed vanilla ice cream,
Swallow the last bit of passion,
Devouring us until there's nothing.

MISSING

I can't notice a star missing in the skies,
But I can notice the sparkle missing in your eyes.

I can't notice a boat missing in the sea,
But I can see the waves that you're being drowned in.

I can't notice a leaf missing on a tree,
But I know you're falling harder than the autumn leaves.

I may not notice a lighthouse has turned off at night,
But I know the flame inside you is slowly burning out.

I know the waves crash the shore away,
But hopefully the memory of me won't fade away someday.

COFFEE

The nice-smelling morning coffee,
That I crave as soon as from the bedsheets I peep,
Maybe it's the way it gets me out of the stance,
Of being half awake and half asleep.

I can feel its effects,
From the moment the sun hits my face,
A burst of energy that's out in the open,
As the caffeine runs through my veins.

The way everything is incorporated,
The coffee, the brown sugar, the milk,
Mixed into a cozy texture,
And hugs my brain as soon as it kicks.

Coffee drips into my cup,
The same way I drip myself into happiness,
The warmth of its presence compensates,
For my cold heart and my loneliness.

It'll always be there for me,
To help me weave my thoughts into rhymes,
To calm my nerves after a long day,
To offer me company late at night.

STRANGER

The name they call me,
Sounds so fake,
The life I'm living,
Feels like a mistake.

I'm inside this body,
Which feels so numb,
I cannot decide,
What my hands should touch.

My eyes see limited sights,
My lips don't say the words I want,
What I say is just an alteration,
Of thoughts that continue to haunt.

My arms are weak, unable to hold on,
My legs walk to the places I hate,
I'm not in charge of my body's control,
I can't bear being unable to think straight.

I WANT MORE

From now on, I want more…

More stargazing in the night sky,
More watching moving clouds,
More friends will whom I go out,
More reasons to be proud,
More looking in the mirror to see my smile,
Instead of my weight or the span of my thighs.

I want more waking up with an intention,
More achievements worthy of mention,
More long-lasting goals,
That will receive my undivided attention.

I want more random smiles,
More giving support than to criticize,
More sparkles in everyone's eyes,
Shortly, I want more life.

NEVER GROW UP

I once was a small ponytailed girl,
With a magical world tiptoeing around her,
Ice cream in hand a shirt sucked in,
Gazing at the dirt on my feet.

Someone so naïve and oblivious,
Curious about this world so mysterious,
Chaotic energy flowing all around,
Colorful fairytales keeping me off the ground.

Back to an age we weren't ashamed,
When we used to be rewarded not blamed,
It would be unpleasant to live another way,
So never grow up, be a kid today.

FABRICS

You weave your feelings in cotton
Lighthearted and cheerful,
Allows you to fully breathe,
But they easily wrinkle and burn you.

Then, you weave your feelings in silk,
That can't be wrinkled in pain,
Strong yet soft and luxurious,
But so hard to get rid of the stains.

Then, you weave your feelings in wool,
Absorbs all the positive thoughts,
But it scratches others skins,
Even though it offers you warmth.

Then, you weave your feelings in leather,
For a cool and modern look,
Attracts everyone around you,
But how cold it's to the touch is overlooked.

So you weave your feelings in polyester,
So that they never fade,
But unable to resist heated situations,
Very burdensome is also the weight.

So you weave your feelings in nylon,
Elastic yet unaffected,
Tough and resilient,
But it's irritating how it generates static.

From Soul to Paper – Krisel Qurku

Then, you weave your feelings in satin,
Standing strong and shiny,
Rich looking and attractive,
Is it worth spending so much for something.

So you cover your feelings in titanium,
Strongly protected from anything outside,
Comfortable in its invincibility,
Until everything gets too hot to bear inside.

Maybe after all, you leave your feelings unprotected and delicate,
Until someone comes along and weaves their feelings with yours,
That would make the best fabric,
That seals the purest kind of bond.

A REMINDER

The one thing I've learned,
Is that we don't always get what we desire in life
In fact it's quite the opposite,
Life is unfair, and that's unchangeable,
And making decisions in this fast paced society has become unimaginably hard,
I even wonder if we have the opportunity to make a decision,
Like it's cut out to be one way or another,
And often this way is the one we despise the most,
Giving up a long-lasting dream is the cost,
That's not easy to pay,
And other times, there is a choice,
That is tempting and fulfilling,
But one that we don't opt for reasons hard to explain,
And maybe for the best of something else,
Or someone else,
Neither choice is fair,
That's something we need to comprehend.
So, if you expect others to treat you well,
Because you treated them well,
You're mistaken,
You can't expect predator not to eat the prey,
Because the prey didn't eat them,
Fairness is just a delusion.
But no matter what comes your way,
Never play the victim,
Never let yourself be taken over by fear,
How else will you learn to face challenges,
Unless you unleash the power within?

MY EYES

I've always asked myself,
If in her eyes,
You will see my eyes,
The eyes that provided you,
Only love and affection,
But you lost those eyes,
Those eyes that longed only for you,
You crave receiving such looks,
And many girls will help you savor it,
But my eyes will remain your favorite.
Full of light and full of life,
Displayed the girl you truly loved,
But someone else will kiss yours,
And fill them with sparkles,
And that's the sight my eyes endure.

TO MY ANXIETY

You took away the relief,
Of breathing freely.

You took away the comfort,
Of sleeping soundly,

You took away the option,
Of making friends easily.

You made the voices in my head,
Scream loudly.

You took away the opportunity,
To learn and explore.

You made me miss out on adventures,
I didn't have the courage to go.

Enough is enough,
It's time I let you go.

WHAT WAS IT LIKE

What was it like,
Before my childlike innocence,
Was turned into chaos and violence.

What was it like,
Before the carelessness and flyaway nature,
Turned into responsibilities and burdens,

What was it like,
Before the screams of laughter,
Was turned into abrupt silence.

What was it like,
Before the enchanted life we lived,
Became a race with society's hurdles.

ACCEPTANCE

You're not a disaster,
You're not a hateful mess,
You are not determined,
By how you look in a tight dress,
What's the point if you like your body,
In some lovely clothes,
But start to hate yourself,
Once you take them off.
You've been criticizing yourself quite a lot,
No good has come out of it,
Try showing your body acceptance,
And use optimism to surround it.
It is not your fault,
For having human legs,
who cares about the faults,
In bone muscle and fat.
This society profits,
By self-hatred and self-doubt,
And rebelling against these principles,
Is a revolutionary art.
Pull to pieces the shame,
You've held on to for so long,
This war with yourself,
Doesn't deserve to go on.

About the author

Born in 2003, Krisel was born and raised in Albania.

From Soul to Paper is her first collection of poetry where she writes about her inspirations over the past four years. Besides her passion for poetry, she aspires to major in computer science and become a successful engineer. According to her, both writing code and writing poetry have some philosophy in common; to make a machine think like a human you have to be able to know and express how humans are themselves.

She writes this collection with the aim of helping readers find solace in her poetry. She wishes the readers to refer to her book in times of easing grief or disappointment by knowing there is always someone who shares the same emotions as they do.

This is

From Soul to Paper

From Soul to Paper – Krisel Qurku

Copyright © 2012 Krisel Qurku

From Soul to Paper

Perspective Press Global Ltd

All rights reserved.

ISBN: 978-1-914275-00-5

www.ingramcontent.com/pod-product-compliance
Lightning Source LLC
Chambersburg PA
CBHW021443080526
44588CB00009B/663